I Like the Seasons!

What Happens in Spring?

Sara L. Latta

Enslow Elementary
an imprint of
 Enslow Publishers, Inc.

40 Industrial Road   PO Box 38
Box 398   Aldershot
Berkeley Heights, NJ 07922   Hants GU12 6BP
USA   UK

http://www.enslow.com

Words to Know

hibernate (HY bur nayt)—To spend the winter sleeping or resting.

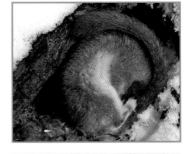

migrate (MY grayt)—To move from one place to another.

season (SEE zuhn)—One of the four parts of the year. Each season has a certain kind of weather.

tilt—To lean to one side.

Earth is tilted.

Contents

What is spring?

Spring is one of the four seasons of the year. The other seasons are summer, fall, and winter. Each season lasts about three months. In spring, signs of warmer weather are everywhere!

summer   fall   winter

4

spring

Why do we have seasons?

Earth goes around the sun. One trip around the sun makes a year. During this trip, Earth **tilts** to one side.

Spring in north part of Earth

North Pole tilts toward the sun; it is summer in the north part of Earth.

Summer

The tilt causes more or less sunlight to fall on different parts of Earth.

Winter

Earth's path around sun

In winter, Earth's North Pole points away from the sun. As Earth moves around the sun, the North Pole begins to tilt toward the sun. This is when spring begins.

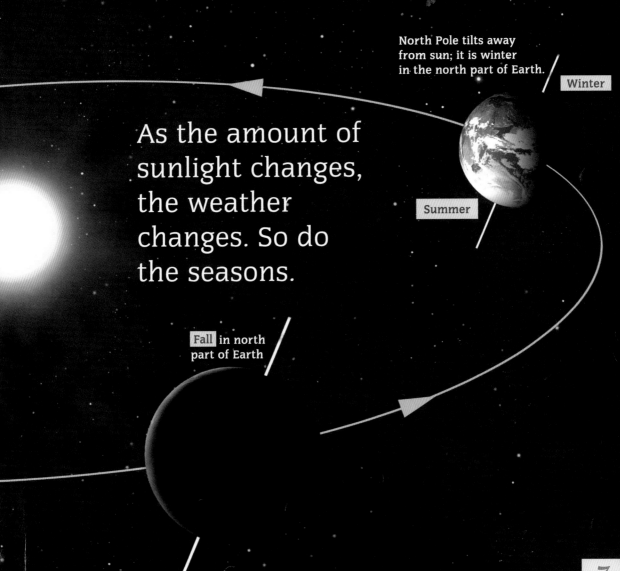

North Pole tilts away from sun; it is winter in the north part of Earth.

Winter

As the amount of sunlight changes, the weather changes. So do the seasons.

Summer

Fall in north part of Earth

When does spring begin?

Spring comes after winter. The first day of spring in the north part of Earth is around March 21.

The north part of Earth slowly gets more heat from the sun. The days begin to get warmer. The days also begin to get longer. There are more hours of sunlight every day.

Spring often brings rainy weather. You may see a rainbow after a spring shower.

What are the first signs of spring?

Warmer, longer days help plants and seeds grow. Flowers pop up to brighten the snow and dark ground. Tiny green leaves appear on the trees. New grass begins to grow again.

What do animals do in the spring?

Animals feel the warmer weather and longer days, too. Animals that hibernate in the winter, like bears, wake up. They are very hungry! They like to eat the young plants that grow in the spring. The food helps them get strong again.

grey squirrel

grizzly bear cub

13

When are animals born?

Many animal babies are born in the spring. The new plants give the babies and their parents fresh food to eat. They will eat and grow during spring and summer.

baby striped skunks

Eastern cottontail
rabbit with babies

Why do animals migrate?

Many animals cannot stay warm or find food in the cold. Where winter weather is too cold, the animals migrate south. It is warmer there.

Snow geese migrate.

When it is warm again in the spring, they migrate back north. The return of the robins is one of the first signs of spring in the north parts of the United States.

American robin, male

What do people do in the spring?

Farmers and gardeners plant seeds in the spring. The rain and warm sun will make their vegetables and flowers grow. Spring has sprung! What will *you* do?

My shadow

  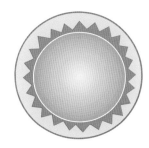

You will need:

- ❖ **sidewalk chalk, 3 colors**
- ❖ **a helper**
- ❖ **a bright sunny day**

1. Pick a bright sunny day. Early in the morning, stand outside in a place that will be sunny all day long. Ask a helper to trace your shadow with sidewalk chalk. Have them trace

20

around your feet so that you can stand in the same spot later on. Lie down next to your shadow. Is it taller or shorter than you are? Where is the sun in the sky?

2. Around noon that same day, stand in the same spot. Ask your friend to trace your shadow with a different color of chalk. How has your shadow changed? Where is the sun now?

3. Do the same thing late in the afternoon. Notice how your shadow changes as the sun moves across the sky.

4. The time of day when your shadow was shortest was when the sun's rays were most direct. During the different seasons, some places on earth get more direct sunlight, and some less direct sunlight.

Learn More

Books

Gibbons, Gail. *The Reasons for Seasons.* New York: Holiday House, 1996.

Rockwell, Anne, and Megan Halsey. *Four Seasons Make a Year.* New York: Walker Publishing Company, 2004.

Schnur, Steven, and Leslie Evans. *Spring: An Alphabet Acrostic.* New York: Clarion Books, 1999.

Simon, Seymour. *Spring Across America.* New York: Hyperion Books for Children, 1996.

Web Sites

Journey North.
  <http://www.learner.org/jnorth/spring2005/index.
  html>

Kids' Crossing.
  <http://www.eo.ucar.edu/kids/index.html>

NASA. *The First Day of Spring.*
  <http://liftoff.msfc.nasa.gov/news/2000/
  news-vernalequinox.asp>

Index

Enslow Elementary, an imprint of Enslow Publishers, Inc.

Enslow Elementary® is a registered trademark of Enslow Publishers, Inc.

Copyright © 2006 by Enslow Publishers, Inc.

All rights reserved.

No part of this book may be reproduced by any means without the written permission of the publisher.

Library of Congress Cataloging-in-Publication Data
Latta, Sara L.
  What happens in spring? / Sara L. Latta.
    p. cm. — (I like the seasons!)
  Includes bibliographical references and index.
  ISBN-10: 0-7660-2419-9 (hardcover)
  1. Spring—Juvenile literature. 2. Seasons—Juvenile literature. I. Title. II. Series
  QB637.5.L38 2006
  508.2-dc22   2005012445

ISBN-13: 978-0-7660-2419-9

Printed in the United States of America
10 9 8 7 6 5 4 3 2

To Our Readers: We have done our best to make sure all Internet Addresses in this book were active and appropriate when we went to press. However, the author and the publisher have no control over and assume no liability for the material available on those Internet sites or on other Web sites they may link to. Any comments or suggestions can be sent by e-mail to comments@enslow.com or to the address on the back cover.

Photo Credits: © 2005 JupiterImages Corporation, p. 4; Adam Jones / Photo Researchers, Inc., p. 8; © age fotostock / SuperStock, pp. 2 (top), 14, 15; © BananaStock / SuperStock, p. 18; © Corel Corporation, pp. 10, 20 (l, r), 22, 23; © Don Paulson / SuperStock, p. 16; © GoodShoot / SuperStock, p. 9; © Kevin Dodge / Masterfile, p. 19; © Lucianne Pashley / SuperStock, p. 5; Mark Garlick/Science Photo Library, pp. 6–7; Michael P. Gadomski / Photo Researchers, Inc., p. 11; © OSF / M. Hamblin / Animals Animals, p. 12; © Phyllis Greenberg / Animals Animals, p. 13; Steve Maslowski / Visuals Unlimited, p. 17; Tom LaBaff, p. 20 (center).

Cover Photo: © Royalty-Free/Corbis

Science Consultant
Harold Brooks, Ph.D.
NOAA/National Severe Storms Laboratory
Norman, Oklahoma

Series Literacy Consultant
Allan A. De Fina, Ph.D.
Past President of the New Jersey Reading Association
Professor, Department of Literacy Education
New Jersey City University

Note to Parents and Teachers: The **I Like the Seasons!** series supports the National Science Education Standards for K–4 science. The Words to Know section introduces subject-specific vocabulary words, including pronunciation and definitions. Early readers may need help with these new words.